21 Ways I'm Able

Kayleigh-louise Wilkinson

BookLeaf Publishing

Presentation by *BookLeaf Publishing*

Web: www.bookleafpub.com

E-mail: info@bookleafpub.com

ISBN: 978-93-95950-39-8

First edition 2022

To the four pieces of my heart that walk around outside of my body

Paul, Katie, Ellie and Joshua

May you always know that any amount pain is worth your happiness, your successes and your victories in life.

PREFACE

To all whom decide to pick up this book and read,

This short collection was never about anything in particular. Wrote at a time in my life when my entire existence was being questioned, I simply wanted to write down one thing each day, for 21 days, that I was grateful for. What transpired, was a collection of poems, each written from the heart, about the things in life that I am grateful for and that define me as a person.

As the book title suggests, these gratitude's are a focus on what I am able to do, in a world where I am told there is so much I shouldn't be able to do. You may see from the jumbled mix before you, I am grateful for a variety of things. Some will be obvious, some a little less so. But all of them are a part of me and I hope that they, in some little way, inspire you to think about what you are grateful for.

Yours in writing,

Kayleigh

I am able to be strong

Strength is my power
It comes from within, deep down
I wield it each day.

I am able to survive

Pain.
Radiating, Encompassing, Infuriating
Tiredness
Exhausting, Debilitating, Never-ending
Memory.
Blurry, Foggy, Infuriating
Migraines.
Pumping, Pounding, Sickening
Depression
Battling, Struggling, Drowning
But here I am, 31 years and 7 months later.
Like a swan, I am paddling furiously below
water whilst attempting to gracefully glide
across a mirrored surface.
It is hard.
But it is a choice.
I am surviving.

I am able to fight

A Recipe to fight when you feel like anything but:

Forgive those who have wronged you, but never forget the lessons learned
Ignite a passion for anything, the light will keep you going in the darkest of times
Go one step further each day, to ensure you never stop
Hate no one, they are not worth the energy you have
Take every opportunity as they come, you never know where it will lead.

I am able to love

My Heart is not whole, but instead broke into five pieces.

One is my husband, who supports me when others would have abandoned long ago.
Two is my first-born, strong and mature beyond her years. She is the one who made me a mother and mirrors my attitude, my temper, my sense of humour and my laugh.
Three is my little girl, second born but second to none. She is witty, clever, poised and caring of all whom are around her.
Four is my son, my last born but never least. He is not what you expect of a little boy, unique in every way and my body aches to protect him.
These four pieces of my heart walk around outside of my body.
The last, piece number five, remains inside of me, waiting to being united with the others every minute of every day.

I feel whole when only the five of us are together.

Laughing
Crying
Talking
Fighting

This is love.

My love is not whole and pretty, it is perfectly broken.

I am able to work

When I grew up, I wanted to dig in the mud.
I wanted to find bones and pottery from years gone by, gently brushing dirt from their hidden graves.
I am grown up.
I don't dig in the mud.
But I do work, hard.
I rally my troops on the battlefield of inequality, fighting the demons in people's pasts and charging forward to create new dreams.
I tell, show and prove to people that they can live whatever life they want, disability and barriers be damned.
I am at the mercy of my body and I can not dig in the mud.
But I have something much better.
I have a passion for my work and I work, hard.

I am able to see

When I can not walk, I look out the window.
I see families, couples and friends enjoying their lives.
I see dogs playing chase and cats playing hide 'n' seek.
I see clouds chasing the sun and the moon, never quite catching up.
Flowers bloom, workers go about their days and children skip merrily by.
When I can not breathe, I look for my husband, lying across from me and count his breaths to calm mine.
When I cannot stand up, I sit and I read new stories that fire my imagination.
My eyes can do so much more than my body and I am blessed to use these when others cannot.

I am able to hear

A simple list, of the things I love to hear.
My name, when you say it
Children laughing
Hedwig's Theme.
Mam, over and over again.
The theme tune to Gilmore Girls.
The washing machine turning
A motorbike engine
A baby gurgling
Birds singing, while the world is quiet.
Rapturous Applause
The tappity tap of a keyboard
Rain on a window
Familiar sounds but still ever so joyful.

I am able to remember

Do you remember when?
I hear those words and I cringe inwardly,
instantly regretting entering whatever
conversation I happen to have ended up in.
I don't remember those tiny insignificant details
I am supposed to, not ever.
I don't remember the neighbours first name and
I don't remember who I sat next to in English
Class that year.
I don't remember how you have your tea or
when we worked with each other at work.
I don't remember if you need your sports kit or
if the permission slip has been signed.
But I do remember what is important.
I remember how scared I was the first time I
held each of you, with the overwhelming
realisation that I was responsible for your entire
wellbeing, without so much as an owners
manual.
I remember the last time I kissed his cold head,
makeup done so well, he could have been
sleeping.
I remember standing at the entrance to the
church, in a dress so tight around my
post-partum body that I thought I might faint,

yet forcing each foot in front of the other to get
to the part where we became one.
I don't remember everything as my head would
hurt.
But I remember who I am and what makes me,
me.

I am able to laugh

Laughter is the best medicine
Or so they say.
But what do you do, when you can't find reason to laugh?
When your pain is to deep
And your heart is too full
That joy doesn't come in the usual ways?
Clear your mind
Clear your heart
Clear your stress, your pain and your weary troubles away
Find small things to be grateful for, to love and to smile at.
The laughter will come back.
I promise.

I am able to be independent

Stubborn as a rock
That's why they say.
And I agree.
I am a rock, hardened by the storm that is my life
It has toughened me and taught me lessons I never wanted to learn
But it has not made me stubborn
It has taught me that where possible
I must be independent.
Independence ensures survival
Independence means I live my life on my terms
Independence is woven into every fibre of my being like the stars weave through the night sky
If you took the stars from the sky,
You would be left with an empty abyss, dark and alone.
Don't take my independence.

I am able to cry

Tears burn and fall
But crying shows how I feel
They mark my journey

I am able to support

When you go to work, what do you do?
Do you nurse the sick or form a fire crew?
Do you watch babies be born or watch over the dead?
Do you fill up your pots and make sure everyone gets fed?
Do you teach our wee bairns to read or to write?
Do you stare hard at a screen, every day and night?
Are you rushed off your feet, clearing dishes and tables?
Or are you buried in straw, mucking out stables?
Do you use lots of tools, like torque bars and wrenches?
Or do you fight for your country, deep in the trenches?
Wherever you are or whatever you do,
My job is to be there, waiting for you
I'll guide and advise you, as you make your life choices
When you are overwhelmed with all of the voices
telling you what to do and what you should be,
Come to me and we'll work through it, you will see

I'll show you the routes, but you will pick one
I'm there to support you, until you are done.
Your life's work is mine too and don't ever
forget,
I'll always be there, even though we just met.

I am able to learn

In my world of books, I don’t walk, I run.
Heavy headed scents of antique paper and polished wood
I can hear the rustling of pages, fingers scanning book spines and the tapping of a pen every so quiet.
Through shelves stacked so very high with stories and journeys I can dip into like a swan dipping their elegant head into the water
If learning was a comfort, it would be my blanket : Warm, familiar, wrapping me up in words and thoughts that are not mine, but still, become part of me.
I yearn for the power that comes with knowledge.
I gasp and gulp for knowledge like a newborn baby gasps for their first breath.
Knowledge is my protector, my sword, my weapon and I yield it with such strength that my body can not muster
It is not just facts that teach me.
Fiction is my friend.
Rowling, Dahl, Blackman, Austen, Gregory, King, Tolkein… The list is endless
Just like the lessons they taught me in life

Learning brings me in from the cold and sits me in front of a roaring fire, with hot cocoa and just a few marshmallows, treating me to the feeling that once I again, I am safe.

I am able to be angry

Anger does not come easily to me
Yet I have much to be angry about.
Why me, why us, why this?
I could ask why, over and over,
Letting it tumble out of my mouth like a waterfall.
But I choose not to.
I choose to let life go on
Until.
Someone hurts us, someone breaks my trust, some abuses my nature
Then the phoenix rises.
It tries to escape my throat like bile,
Burning and scalding as it rushes out
I don't trust easy and when that's broken,
Anger consumes me.
Anger at them for betraying me so
Anger at myself for letting my guard down
I don't get angry easily, but when I do, I feel like a force to be reckoned with.
I choose to get angry, only when needed.
It reminds me that I am strong.

I am able to protect

Protection comes in many forms
Whilst sometimes distant, it often swarms
Around your body, ready to defend
Where it will fight until the end.

I offer my protection to you, in every way
That in the future, there will come a day
Where you will look back, a tear in your eye
And know I was always prepared to die

If it promised your happiness or ensure your health,
If it offered you love or provided you wealth.
As a mother I will fight to the death for you,
no questions, because that is what we do.

I offer my protection, until the day it's not needed,
Until another takes my place and I am succeeded.
I know they will never protect you as much as I can,
But that by this time you will protect your own, that is the plan.

I am able to grow a child

27 months.
117 weeks.
821 days.
I carried you all; nourished you, fed you, grew you.
I cried over your name choices
I spent hours choosing your crib
I laboured over every decision that might affect you.
My body crumbled under the pressure, but did so to sustain you.
When I couldn't walk, it was to ensure you would.
With every painful breath, I was grateful that you were breathing and would cry when you entered the world.
Whilst you grow outside of me now,
Please.
Remember.
You grew inside of me for those first precious nine months and I will watch you blossom, like a sunflower stretching for light.
I will always be there for you.

I am able to inspire

I am able to inspire

Inspiration doesn't always come from
unbelievable events.
Many young children wanted to be astronauts
when man walked on the moon.
But more young children have become teachers
after their own teacher showed them knowledge
which inspired their hearts
More people have become nurses and doctors
because of a kind soul who took care of them
Adults have retrained as counsellors more often
than not, because of the supportive words of a
friend
Inspiration comes from the everyday acts
Holding open a door inspires someone else to be
kind
Supporting a friend inspires that same person to
support another
Raising money for a charity inspires
communities to get involved
Inspiration is in the acts you do and the words
you speak
What can you inspire today?

I am able to write

Blank pages need words
Just like we need air to breath
See a page and write

I am able to be confident

You won't find me in the makeup box,
Or the salon up the road,
I'm not in the way you flip your hair,
Or on the motorbike you rode.

I'm not on the designer handbag
That you brought last week online,
I don't hide amongst the big name brands,
Like Dolce or Calvin Klein,

I don't drive around in sports cars,
That average joe couldn't buy,
Or fly away in jumbo jets,
As they zoom across the sky.

Yes, these are the places that most would look,
But you'd be surprised where I start,
I don't come from materialistic things,
I come from in your heart.

I'm there in the shine of your eyes,
When you carry a secret inside,
I'm the calm you feel when you sit at the beach
And watch the watery tide.
I'm the knowledge that you are loved,

By one so special to you,
The feeling of warmth when you know deep inside,
That your wishes will come true.

True confidence comes from happiness,
Inner calm and serenity,
Confidence is there for us all to achieve,
If we stop chasing it and let it be.

I am able to be me

Harry Potter
Hot Coffee's
Cold mornings, with your breath in the air.
Roast Beef
Seaside visits
Childhood rides and a trip to the fair
Movie nights
Cuddly blankets
A bucket of popcorn we can share
Summer flowers
Barbeque afternoons
The smell of the church when sat down for prayer
A new book
Firework displays
Christmas eve and the creak of the stair
Rainy Days
All hallows eve and the threat of a scare
Long hot soaks
Snow on the ground
The love in your eyes when you show me you care
These are the things that make me unique
We are all individual, like the days of the week

I am able to define who I am

There are many ways that I am not able.

I cannot run like the athletes I see in the
Olympics, nor the everyday people in the park.
I cannot move without wincing, like I watch
those around me do every day.
I cannot wear a size 6 dress to a party, like all
the pretty girls I see.
I cannot sing and charm the birds from the tree,
nor paint a picture with colours from the
rainbow.
I cannot live pain free, nor can I can breathe
without worrying it will be my last.
I cannot see my future, for much is unknown
and I certainly do not know how long I have.

But my 'cannots' do not define who I am.
I define myself by what I am able to do.

I am strong and my strength is unbreakable.
I will survive, no questions asked.
I will fight to the end.
I love hard.
I work for the better of our communities.
I see past barriers.

I hear what your heart wants to tell me.
I remember what is needed and make memories for the future.
I laugh loud.
I am independent and protect my right to do things on my own.
I cry real tears.
I support without receiving.
I learn whatever and whenever I can.
I get angry but that's okay.
I will protect fiercely.
I grew my children and now pieces of my heart walk outside of my body.
I strive to inspire with every action.
I write for my own therapy.
I am confident in everything I do.
I am me, unapologetically.
I define who I am; Independent, Strong Willed and Fighting. Always.

These are what I am able to do and this is what defines me.

What can you do?

www.ingramcontent.com/pod-product-compliance
Lightning Source LLC
Chambersburg PA
CBHW051753130826
49812CB00033B/1136
* 9 7 8 9 3 9 5 9 5 0 3 9 8 *